Jesus with Us

The Gift of the Eucharist

Written by Anthony Tarzia
Illustrated by Julian Ferri

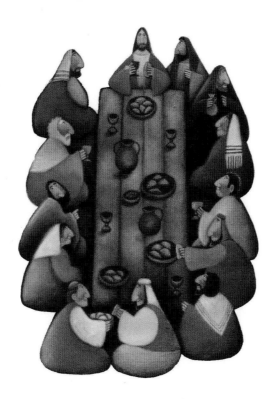

Pauline
BOOKS & MEDIA

Boston

Nihil Obstat: Very Rev. Timothy J. Shea, V. F.
Imprimatur: ✠ Bernard Cardinal Law
July 6, 1995

Library of Congress Cataloging-in-Publication Data

Tarzia, Antonio.
   [Primo incontro con Gèsu. English]
   Jesus with us: the gift of the Eucharist / by Antonio Tarzia; illustrated by Julian Ferri.
      p.   cm.
   Summary: A history of the Eucharist, that sacrament of the Catholic Church in which, by partaking of bread and wine, one receives the body and blood of Jesus.
   ISBN 0-8198-4781-X (pbk.)
   1. Lord's Supper—Catholic Church—Juvenile literature. 2. Lord's Supper—History—Juvenile literature. [1. Lord's Supper—Catholic Church. 2. Sacraments—Catholic Church.] I. Ferri, Julian, ill. II. Title.
   BX2215.2.T3713   1996
   232.9'57—dc20
                                   96-40443
                                       CIP
                                     AC

Scripture quotations from the *Good News Bible*
   Old Testamant, copyright © American Bible Society, 1976
   New Testament: copyright © American Bible Society, 1966, 1971, 1976

Original title: *Il Primo Incontro con Gèsu*

Copyright© 1993, Edizione Paoline, Piazza Soncino, 5, 20092 Cinisello Balsamo, Milan, Italy

Graphics: Rosa Elena Polastri

Translated from the Italian by Concetta Belleggia, FSP

Edited by Anne Eileen Heffernan, FSP

Published by Pauline Books & Media, 50 Saint Pauls Avenue, Boston MA 02130-3491

Printed in the U.S.A.

JWU KSEUSAHUDNHA4-241016 4781-X

www.pauline.org

Pauline Books & Media is the publishing house of the Daughters of St. Paul, an international congregation of women religious serving the Church with the communications media.

10 11 12 13 14 15   19 18 17 16 15 14

Introduction

We are always meeting people. We meet some people only once in a while. We meet others, like our good friends, very often. We might meet some people every day on the bus. We might see other people at church. Sometimes we get to know a person quickly and become friends right away.

Our meeting with Jesus is a meeting with a friend. Jesus will be our Friend for our whole life! We can tell Jesus about whatever makes us feel happy or sad. He understands. Jesus knows all about us. Jesus loves us.

First Communion is a special meeting with Jesus. It's a very important meeting. It's a beautiful celebration that shows we are on the way to becoming grown-up followers of Jesus. Jesus invites us to a special meal. In sharing this meal we become closer friends of Jesus—just like Peter, Andrew, and John. These close friends of Jesus shared many meals with him.

Bread and Wine

After God made the world, he told the very first people to take good care of it. God told the people to farm the land, so that it would give them good food to eat.[1]

The earth pays farmers back for their hard work. In the summer, golden wheat grows in the fields. In the fall, sweet bunches of grapes grow on grapevines. From wheat, people make bread. From grapes, people make wine.

But it takes hard work to help the wheat and grapes to grow. God told the first people, "You will have to work hard and sweat to make the soil produce anything."[2]

But even though work is hard, it makes us happy. We see what we can do. We think of how wonderfully God made us. And God wants us to be happy. The Bible tells us, "Eat your food and be happy; drink your wine and be cheerful."[3]

Bread is simple food, but very important. People share bread with each other to show that they are friends. People share bread with guests and with travelers who are hungry and tired. Bread makes travelers feel strong again. Bread makes travelers feel welcome. When people find bread, they feel "at home."

The Sacrifice of Abraham

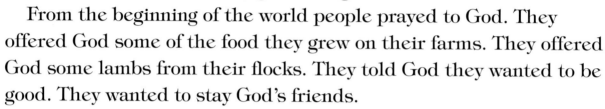

God gave people the whole world to live in. He put people in charge of the world. He called people his friends. What could people give back to God after God had done so many good things for them?

From the beginning of the world people prayed to God. They offered God some of the food they grew on their farms. They offered God some lambs from their flocks. They told God they wanted to be good. They wanted to stay God's friends.

The Bible is the oldest holy book of the people who believe in one God. In the Bible, the Jewish people, the Christian people, and the Muslim people read about people who gave gifts to God. These gifts are called sacrifices. The Bible tells us that Cain and Abel offered sacrifices to God.[4] The Bible tells us that Abraham almost offered his son Isaac to God. But God did not let Abraham sacrifice Isaac. God showed Abraham that he did not want human sacrifices. God does not want innocent people to be killed.[5]

In the Bible we also read about Melchisedek. Melchisedek was a king and a priest. One time, Abraham came back from a war as a winner. King Melchisedek went to see him. He gave Abraham some bread and wine. Then Melchisedek blessed Abraham.[6]

Bread and wine are ordinary food for many people. In some religions bread and wine are offered to God as sacrifices.

Jonah, the Boy with the Fish

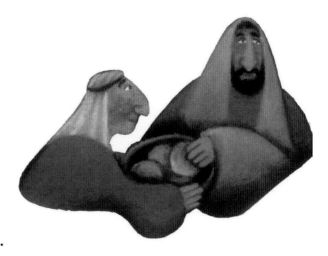

This is a story about a boy who lived at the time of Jesus. We will call him Jonah. One day, Jonah was on his way to see his brothers. His brothers were watching their herd of camels. Jonah was bringing them something to eat. In his sack he was carrying five loaves of fresh bread and two fish that had been dried in the sunlight.

As he walked down the road, Jonah saw a huge crowd of people. The people were listening to a teacher. The teacher was Jesus. Jonah stopped to listen—partly because he was tired and partly because he was curious. He forgot that it was already afternoon.

The people were getting very hungry. Andrew, a friend of Jesus, called to Jonah, "What are you carrying in that sack?" "Five loaves of bread and two fish," Jonah answered. Jonah offered the precious bag to Andrew. Jesus' friends asked each other, "What can we do with only five loaves of bread for all these people?" But, just the same, they brought the sack to Jesus.

Jesus took the loaves of bread. He thanked God, his Father, for them. Then Jesus told his friends to give the bread to the people who were sitting on the grass. Jesus did the same with the fish. The people ate as much bread and fish as they wanted.[7]

There were more than five thousand people there that day. But they all had enough of Jonah's bread and fish to eat! This wonderful thing that Jesus did makes us think of the Holy Eucharist, which Jesus would give to all his friends at the Last Supper.

The Last Supper

On Passover night the Jewish people eat special bread and drink wine. The Passover is an important anniversary. The Jewish people thank God for setting them free from slavery in Egypt.[8] God did wonderful things to set his people free. That event which happened to the ancestors of the Jewish people becomes an event in their own lives today.

Jesus celebrated the Passover every year. On the night before Jesus died on the cross, he ate his last Passover with his friends. He wanted to celebrate the wonderful things God had done for his people in Egypt. But Jesus wanted to give another meaning to the celebration, too. Jesus wanted to leave us a very special gift.

While Jesus was eating with his friends, he took a large piece of bread. He said a prayer of blessing. Then Jesus broke the bread. He gave it to his disciples. Jesus said: "Take and eat it: *this is my Body.*" Next Jesus took the cup. He said another prayer of thanks. Jesus passed the cup to his disciples. He said: "Drink it, all of you: *this is my Blood,* which seals God's covenant, my Blood poured out for many for the forgiveness of sins."[9]

The friends of Jesus did what he told them to do. Later, they repeated this again and again. Today, through the Church, people still receive the Body and Blood of Jesus. Jesus' Body and Blood look and taste like bread and wine. They are called the sacrament of the Eucharist. (Eucharist means "giving thanks.") A sacrament is a sign that God is present in a special way to do something in our lives. The Eucharist makes the death of Jesus present today. By his death Jesus gives us his own life. We call that life "grace."

The Death of Jesus

Jesus once said, "The greatest love a person can have for his friends is to give his life for them."[10] Jesus did that for all of us.

During his last Passover supper Jesus washed his friends' feet. (Jesus wanted to teach his friends to help others and not to think that they were better than others.) Then Jesus said a prayer of thanks to God. This special supper was the last one that Jesus shared with his friends. That is why we call it the Last Supper.

Jesus changed the bread and wine into his Body and Blood. He had promised to do this. Once he had told his friends, "I am the living bread that came down from heaven. If anyone eats this bread, he will live forever. The bread that I will give him is my flesh, which I give so that the world may live."[11]

The day after the Last Supper, Roman soldiers brought Jesus to a hill called Calvary outside the city of Jerusalem. The soldiers killed Jesus there by nailing him to a wooden cross. This was called crucifixion.

In those days, crucifixion was the worst way a person could be killed. It was a cruel punishment. And Jesus did not deserve to be punished. He was God's own Son.[12]

After the time of Jesus, the cross became a sign of God's love for people. That is why we see crosses on churches. That is why we always see a cross near the altar where the priest celebrates the Eucharist.

In every Mass Jesus does just what he did during the Last Supper. In every Mass Jesus offers his death and resurrection to his Father in heaven. Jesus does this so that all the people in the world can go to heaven.

The Disciples of Emmaus

After Jesus died on the cross, his friends placed him in a tomb. Some soldiers rolled a heavy stone in front of his tomb. It really seemed that Jesus' life had been a failure.

Jesus had friends called disciples. Disciples are people who "follow" a particular teacher. Jesus' disciples were very sad because Jesus had died. Two of the disciples were going back to their village. The village was called Emmaus. Emmaus was about seven miles away from Jerusalem. It was a long walk. As they walked along, the disciples talked about Jesus. Then the disciples saw a man coming up behind them. The traveler joined them. He listened to what they were saying. They told him about Jesus' death and what people were saying about it. Then the traveler started to talk. He said that according to the Bible, Jesus had to die, but that Jesus also had to rise from the dead "to enter his glory."[13] He explained the Bible to them.

It was late when the three of them got to the village. It was getting dark. The disciples invited the traveler to spend the night with them. The man said yes. So they all went into the house.

While the unknown man was sitting at table with the disciples, he took the bread, said a prayer of thanks, broke the bread, and gave it to them. The eyes of the two men became big. They recognized Jesus! But right away Jesus disappeared.[14]

This true story was written by St. Luke. There are many stories about what Jesus said and did after he rose from the dead. But this story is special. This story is like the Mass. At Mass we listen to and think about some words from the Bible. There are prayers to thank God. Then there is the breaking of the bread. And most important of all, Jesus is there.

Meeting to Break the Bread

One day Jesus went back to heaven. Soon he sent the Holy Spirit to help his disciples, the first Christians.[15] The first Christians used to have meetings. They would talk about what Jesus their teacher had done when he lived with them. Sometimes Mary was with them. Mary was Jesus' Mother. She had rocked Jesus as a baby at Bethlehem. She had stood beside Jesus while he was hanging from the cross. Mary had cried to see Jesus suffering.

Mary remembered many special things that had happened. She remembered what the angel had said when he asked her to become Jesus' mother.[16] Mary remembered what an old man named Simeon had said when he held baby Jesus in his arms in the temple of Jerusalem.[17] Mary told all these stories to the first Christians.

The Christians used to end their meetings with the breaking of the bread by a man who today we would call a priest. (Today we call this the Eucharistic Celebration or Mass.) At that time, Mass was at night. St. Luke tells us about one of these celebrations. It took place in the city of Troas, while St. Paul was there.

St. Luke tells us: "On Saturday evening we gathered together for the fellowship meal. Paul spoke to the people and kept on speaking until midnight, since he was going to leave the next day. . . . A young man named Eutychus was sitting in the window, and as Paul kept on talking, Eutychus got sleepier and sleepier, until he finally went sound asleep and fell from the third story to the ground. When they picked him up, he was dead. But Paul went down and threw himself on him and hugged him. 'Don't worry,' he said, 'he is still alive!' Then he went back upstairs, broke bread, and ate. After talking with them for a long time, even until sunrise, Paul left. They took the young man home alive and were greatly comforted."[18]

Mass in the Catacombs

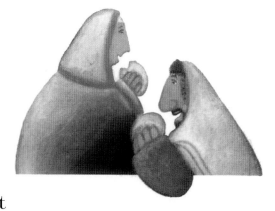

The first Christians did not have churches. They celebrated the Eucharist in their homes after work. Sometimes, to get away from curious people or from people who wanted to hurt them, they went down to the catacombs. The catacombs were underground cemeteries. These cemeteries were common in many cities. In the catacombs the Christians listened to the reading of the Gospel. "Gospel" means the Good News about what Jesus did and said. The Christians knew that Jesus had come on earth to teach us that all men, women, and children are very special. Jesus taught that we are very special because God loves each of us with a good father's heart.

Other people who heard this Good News were excited. They wanted to be baptized. They knew that once they were baptized they would be Christians too. And when they were Christians they could do more than just listen to the reading of the Word of God. They could take part in the breaking of the bread, the celebration of the Eucharist. They could receive the Body and Blood of Jesus.

When the priest broke the bread, he repeated the words that Jesus had used during the Last Supper. St. Paul said this in a letter to his friends. St. Paul wrote: "The Lord Jesus on the night he was betrayed, took a piece of bread, gave thanks to God, broke it, and said, 'This is my body, which is for you. Do this in memory of me.' In the same way, after the supper he took the cup and said: 'This cup is God's new covenant sealed with my blood. Whenever you drink it, do so in memory of me.'"[19]

A Fish Carrying Bread

Today when Jesus' followers visit Rome, they might go to see the catacombs and other places where the bodies of the first Christians were buried. If they do, they will see something special. There are pictures carved in the stones. There are also beautiful paintings on the walls. Some of these carvings and paintings show peacocks and palm branches. These symbols stand for Jesus' rising from the dead. Other pictures stand for the Eucharist. There might be a lamb with a cross, a cup, a bunch of grapes, some wheat, or even a fish carrying a basket full of bread.

The fish has a very important meaning. It stands for Jesus. This is because the letters of the Greek word for "fish" (i-c-t-u-s) are initials for a short prayer of faith used by the first Christians. This is the prayer: Jesus Christ, Son of God, Savior.

In the catacombs we also find pictures of some wonderful things that Jesus did which remind us of the Eucharist. There are pictures of Jesus multiplying the bread and fish. Other pictures show the wedding at Cana. Jesus and his mother, Mary, were there. When the party ran out of wine, Jesus changed water into wine.[20]

Sometimes the Roman leaders wanted to kill the Christians because they wouldn't worship the emperor or pagan gods. At those times, Christians would celebrate the Eucharist in the hidden underground rooms of the catacombs.

Great Experts on the Eucharist

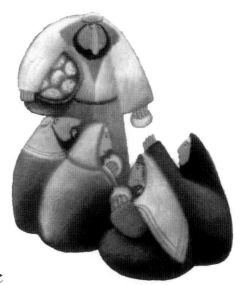

An expert is a person who knows a lot about something. Experts about God are called theologians. The first great expert on the Eucharist was St. Paul. Paul once wrote some letters to the Christians in the city of Corinth. He told the people how Jesus gave us the Eucharist. Paul taught the people how to celebrate the Eucharist better. Paul said that the Eucharist is the new sacrifice offered to God in memory of the death and resurrection of Jesus.[21]

St. Augustine was another great theologian of the Eucharist. He was the bishop of a place called Hippo. St. Augustine said that the Eucharist can really change us when we receive It the way Jesus wants us to. St. Augustine also said that the Eucharist brings everyone in the Church together. In a mysterious way, the Church is the Mystical Body of the risen Jesus.

Over seven hundred years ago, some theologians held meetings to talk about how Jesus is really present under the appearances of bread and wine. The person who explained this best was St. Thomas Aquinas. He said, "By the power of the sacrament, Jesus is present in his suffering, dying and rising, and Christians offer themselves

to God together with Jesus." St. Thomas explained that even though we cannot see it happen, we know that in the Mass the bread and wine become Jesus' own Body and Blood.

The Miracle of Bolsena

In the year 1263, Pope Urban IV was the head of Jesus' Church. He lived in the city of Orvieto in Italy. One day a priest from Germany came to see Pope Urban. The priest told the pope about something wonderful that had happened to him. This is the story: The priest was sad because he couldn't believe that Jesus is really present in the Holy Eucharist. Then one day he was celebrating Mass in a church in the town of Bolsena. Something amazing happened. When the priest broke the Host, it started to bleed—right in front of everyone's eyes! A lot of blood fell into the chalice. The blood even stained a large part of the corporal. (The corporal is a white cloth that is placed on the altar during Mass.)

When Pope Urban heard this, he sent the bishop of Orvieto to find out if the story was really true. It was! Then the pope told the bishop to bring the broken Host and stained corporal to Orvieto. Today they are kept in the beautiful cathedral there. Many people visit that cathedral to pray.

Around that time, the Church began to celebrate the feast of the Body and Blood of Jesus Christ. People held processions (special parades to honor God). The Holy Eucharist was placed inside a very beautiful holder called a monstrance. The monstrance had a little window in it so that all the people could see the Host. The priest carried the Holy Eucharist through the crowded city. The people bowed their heads as the monstrance passed them. They threw flowers on the ground. This was a way of showing their faith that Jesus was present and that they loved him.

The Second Vatican Council

About four hundred years ago, some people started to doubt that Jesus was really present in the Eucharist. The pope and the bishops called a meeting to see how they could help these people. This big meeting was called the Council of Trent. This is what the pope and bishops told all the people at the end of the meeting: "In the most holy sacrament of the Eucharist is contained truly, really, and substantially the Body and Blood, the soul and the divinity of our Lord Jesus Christ, therefore Jesus Christ whole and entire. In every little piece of the Host and in every drop of the consecrated wine the whole Lord is mysteriously present, human and divine."[22]

There was another special meeting of the pope and bishops from 1962 to 1965. This meeting was called the Second Vatican Council. At the Second Vatican Council, the pope and bishops made some changes in the Mass. They did this to make our Eucharistic Celebration more like the Mass celebrated by the first Christians. These changes made it easier for people to take part in the Mass.

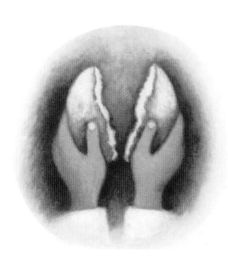

In the Mass we say or sing many prayers together. One is the "Amen." Our "Amen" shows that we want to do everything that God asks us to. Saying "Amen" together also helps us to feel close to our brothers and sisters in our parish and in Jesus' Church all over the world.

God's People Celebrate Eucharist

Before the Second Vatican Council, the priest did not face the people when he celebrated Mass. That made it hard for people to really take part in the celebration. They could only watch the priest. But now the priest faces us. It is easier for us to join in the celebration of the Eucharist. Before the Second Vatican Council, the Mass was always celebrated in the Latin language. But today not very many people understand Latin. So now each priest can celebrate Mass in whatever language the people understand.

At Mass we celebrate the Good News that by dying and rising Jesus gave us the chance to live with God forever. We share our joy with one another. During the celebration the priest invites us to give each other the sign of peace. This sign means that we all belong to Jesus' Church. It means that we also belong to one another.

At Mass the first two readings from the Bible are proclaimed by the lectors. The priest or a deacon reads the third Bible reading, which is the Gospel—the Good News. In the Prayer of the Faithful

we pray for the needs and problems of the whole world. During the presentation of the gifts we bring the bread and the wine to God's altar. We also offer God our feelings—happy or sad. At Communion time we receive the Body and Blood of Jesus in the Eucharist. Jesus comes to us to make us strong believers.

The Eucharist in Our Life

The Mass does not end when we leave the church. The Eucharistic Celebration gives us special strength. It helps us to be strong and good like Jesus. It helps us to love others, to serve them, to tell the truth, and to be generous. We find happiness at every Eucharistic Celebration because that is where we meet Jesus. Jesus died for us and rose from the dead for us. Jesus becomes present among us at Mass because he loves us so much.

Jesus wants us to share our happiness with our friends and neighbors. Jesus wants us to share with everyone the happiness that he gives us!

The Eucharist is the food that helps us to live as Jesus lived. By living like Jesus, we can give good example to other people. Jesus said: "By this everyone will know that you are my disciples, if you have love for one another."[23]

The Eucharist is not a ceremony celebrated in memory of Jesus. It is a sacrament. It is the loving presence of Jesus. It really changes

us. It helps us to change this world into the best world possible. Changing the whole world is a big project, but if we work together with Jesus, we can do it!

Notes

[1] See Genesis 2:15.

[2] Genesis 3:19.

[3] Ecclesiastes 9:7.

[4] See Genesis 4:3–4.

[5] See Genesis 22:1–18.

[6] See Genesis 14:18–20.

[7] John 6:1–13.

[8] See Exodus 12:1–14.

[9] Matthew 26:26–28.

[10] John 15:13.

[11] John 6:51.

[12] See Matthew 27:27–54.

[13] Luke 24:26.

[14] See Luke 24:13–34.

[15] See Acts 1:1–11; 2:1–4.

[16] See Luke 1:26–38.

[17] See Luke 2:25–35.

[18] See Acts 20:7–12.

[19] 1 Corinthians 11:23–25.

[20] See John 2:1–11.

[21] See 1 Corinthians 11:23–26.

[22] Council of Trent: *Decree on the Eucharist*, October 11, 1551, canon 1.

[23] John 13:35.